MELBOURNE

Melbourne, capital of the State of Victoria, is home to more than three million people who blend Australian origins and culture with the customs and cultures of many other lands. Once settled in this gracious city, or in its wide-ranging, well-tailored suburbs, a newcomer rapidly becomes a Melburnian, a type of Australian whose characteristics are defined by life in one of the world's loveliest cities, where many nineteenth-century buildings stand in stately glory amongst the shining towers of today's commerce.

Culture and art are important in Victoria's capital, and the cosmopolitan nature of the Melburnian and the city's many visitors ensure that the attractions range from the most sophisticated of events to crowd-pleasing street entertainments.

Melburnians enjoy sharing their city and its bounty, and every month of the year offers special delights. These include January's Australian Open Tennis, February's St Kilda Festival, March's 10-day Moomba Festival and the Formula One Grand Prix at the Albert Park circuit, June's International Film Festival, the Melbourne International Festival in October, the Spring Racing Carnival (climaxing in November with the Melbourne Cup), December's Carols by Candlelight, and much more. And, of course, there's always Australian Rules Football... a great game that originated in Melbourne, stirs the Melburnian's soul, and has been generously given to the world.

Melbourne is a beautiful city of grace and charm, offering places aplenty to relax and enjoy nature's gifts, from the multitude of parks and gardens to the placid Yarra River and the shores and waters of Port Phillip Bay.

Above: *A view of Melbourne looking east from the Rialto Observation Deck, with the Yarra River on the right.*
Below: *West Melbourne and Docklands, looking over Colonial Stadium and the Bolte Bridge.*

Above: *The view from the Rialto Observation Deck over the Yarra River and Crown Casino to Port Phillip Bay.*

MARVELLOUS MELBOURNE

Melbourne is Australia's second-largest city, home to over seventy per cent of Victorians, and a cosmopolitan centre that lives up to its motto: *"We gather strength as we grow"*. In the second half of the nineteenth century, wealth from gold and from Victoria's rural riches financed the construction of buildings that are architectural gems of their period. In the city centre, these legacies of a gracious age stand beside glittering, glass-sheathed commercial towers, symbolising the way in which Melbourne's gracious colonial traditions co-exist with the city's vigorous modern lifestyle. Melburnians have been wise enough to preserve their heritage while incorporating the best from other cultures: today the city is in the forefront of commerce, industry and the arts. Twenty-first century Melbourne, proudly astride the Yarra River, is one of the great cities of the world.

Above: *The Yarra, looking downstream towards Princes Bridge.*

MELBOURNE'S MIRROR, THE YARRA

It is nearly 240 kilometres from the Yarra River's source in the Baw Baws to its mouth at Port Melbourne. Along the way, it waters upland forests and rocky hills, then flows across wide river flats, once tranquil pasture, but now increasingly urban. The final stages of the Yarra, through Melbourne city, are bordered by parks, gardens and a multitude of places where people meet to enjoy themselves. Pleasure craft, rowers and canoeists cruise the river, while cyclists and walkers use its banks.

Above: *(Left) The city reflected in the Yarra at dawn. (Right) The view downstream from Princes Bridge.*
Below: *The Yarra at night, with Spencer Street Bridge on the right.*

Above: *Flinders Street Station.*

Below: *(Left) The Yarra carries cruise boats and pleasure craft. (Right) The City Circle tram stops at attractions throughout the city.*

GETTING AROUND MELBOURNE

There are many ways of getting around Melbourne city and its far-flung suburbs. Though a car is useful, a tram lets the explorer see the city in traditional style: the Colonial Tramcar Restaurant offers a night tour, while free City Circle trams pass many city sights. The City Explorer bus allows patrons to view the city and get on or off at 16 special stops, while the City Wanderer ventures outside the city centre. River cruises are based near Princes Bridge; nearby Flinders Street Station is the hub of the metropolitan rail network. Heritage walks criss-cross the city, and much of Melbourne's unique architecture merits the close inspection that only a leisurely stroll can allow.

Top: *Melbourne's trams are a popular means of getting about city and suburbs.*
Above: *A pair of horses and an elegant carriage provide a wonderful way to see the city.*

Above left and clockwise: *A view down the Yarra from the Princes Bridge end of Southgate; the spire of the Theatres Building glitters beyond this Southgate statue; looking from Southgate across to Flinders Walk and Flinders Street Station; Southgate entrance with Ophelia, by Deborah Halpern, on right; sculpture at Southgate.*

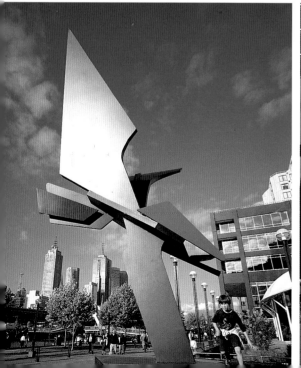

Above: *Entertainers amuse the crowd at Southgate.*

SPARKLING SOUTHGATE

Just across the river from the city centre is the Southgate Arts and Leisure Precinct, a fascinating complex of shops, galleries, places to eat and sculpture-ornamented riverside spaces. The riverside walkways attract crowds to promenade or watch the street performers. Food from all over the world is available from its international food hall, restaurants and cafés. It is a short walk down the river's verge from Southgate to the Crown Entertainment Complex, while the Victorian Arts Centre is just around the corner in St Kilda Road. A footbridge links Southgate to Flinders Walk and Flinders Street Station, and river cruises depart from Southgate and nearby Princes Walk.

MELBOURNE AT NIGHT

As dusk falls on Melbourne, the city becomes a place of bright lights and welcoming venues where people gather to talk, eat and enjoy themselves. The city centre offers gourmet delights in areas such as Chinatown, as well as myriad theatres, clubs, pubs and bistros. Close by, Southgate, the Arts Centre and inner suburbs such as Richmond, Carlton and Fitzroy are enduring attractions.

Top: *(Left) The entrance to Chinatown. (Right) Parliament Gardens with the Princess Theatre to the right.*
Above: *A view from Kings Domain, past the statue of the Marquis of Linlithgow to the lights of the city.*
Opposite: *The facade of the Crown Entertainment Complex, largest casino in the Southern Hemisphere.*

Above and below: *The Museum of Victoria (above) and an IMAX Theatre (below left) are sited near the Royal Exhibition Building in Carlton Gardens. (Below right) Angel, by Deborah Halpern, stands outside the Victorian National Gallery.*

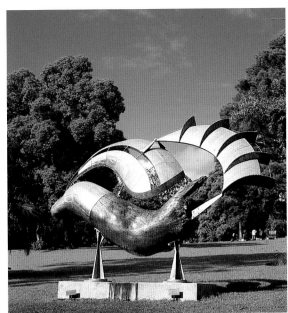

Top: (Left) Melbourne's public gardens are galleries of sculptures and statues. (Right) Street artist at work.
Above: Sculptures ornament the promenade that runs along the south bank of the Yarra River.

MELBOURNE ON DISPLAY

Since the gold rush days of the mid nineteenth century, Melbourne has been a centre for the visual arts, and today galleries and exhibitions abound. Sculptures enrich the many parks and gardens; artworks overflow formal premises and decorate the streets.

In St Kilda Road, the National Gallery of Victoria exhibits impressive international collections as well as Aboriginal and other Australian works. Many entertaining and educational hours can be spent at the Museum of Victoria, which occupies a striking complex on the north side of the Royal Exhibition Building in Carlton. Other rewarding galleries are the Australian Centre for Contemporary Art on Dallas Brooks Drive and the Museum of Modern Art at Heide, in Bulleen, an outer suburb.

THE PERFORMING ARTS

In Melbourne, the world's greatest actors, musicians and other stars can be appreciated in settings worthy of their talents. The Arts Centre, just over Princes Bridge from the city, contains a Concert Hall, home of the Melbourne Symphony Orchestra, and a Theatres Building, where productions range from grand opera to puppet plays. For those who enjoy musicals, Her Majesty's, the Regent and the Princess stage big productions, while among more intimate theatres are the Malthouse in Southbank, La Mama and the Courthouse in Carlton, the Playbox in South Melbourne, and Chapel off Chapel in Prahran. Theatreworks in Acland Street, St Kilda, specialises in community theatre. Clubs, pubs, theatre restaurants and the malls and streets feature all manner of performers. Melbourne's International Comedy Festival begins as close as possible to the 1st of April each year.

Above: *The Victorian Arts Centre, consisting of the Concert Hall and the Theatres Building, is close to the Yarra River and Southgate.*

Above: *The Theatres Building of the Victorian Arts Centre.*
Below: *(Left) A juggler outside the Arts Centre, St Kilda Road. (Right) Street performers in Acland Street, St Kilda.*

Above: *(Left) Ned Kelly's armour at Old Melbourne Gaol. (Right) Captain Cook's statue stands outside his parents' cottage in Fitzroy Gardens.*

LEGACIES

Heritage Walks are an energetic but entertaining way to picture Melbourne's past, and there are plenty of National Trust-listed places to enjoy. (The National Trust, Tasma Terrace, East Melbourne, will provide information on the city's many historic sites.)

Old Melbourne Gaol, built in 1841 and a place of execution until 1929, reflects some of the grimmer side of the city's history and features Ned Kelly memorabilia. Governor La Trobe's Cottage served as Government House until 1872. It stands near the Shrine of Remembrance in Kings Domain. Another colonial structure, Como House in South Yarra, built between 1840 and 1859, gives a glimpse into the lives of nineteenth-century gentry. For the nautically minded, a visit to the Polly Woodside Maritime Museum near Spencer Street Bridge is well worth while.

Top left and clockwise: *The Hotel Windsor (opened 1883); the Polly Woodside (launched in 1885); Como House (dates from 1847); Parliament House (built in 1856); Melbourne City Baths (built in 1903); Governor La Trobe's cottage (assembled in 1840).*

Above: *The Royal Exhibition Building in Carlton Gardens was erected in 1880.*
Below: *(Left) St Pauls Cathedral. (Right) The Shot Tower, built in 1889, is preserved in Melbourne Central.*

Above: *The Eternal Flame burns in front of the Shrine of Remembrance in Kings Domain.*

MEMORABLE MELBOURNE

Some of Melbourne's buildings stay in the memory either because of their architectural excellence or because of the reason for their construction. Melbourne's Shrine of Remembrance in Kings Domain was erected as a memorial to the dead of World War I and incorporates monuments to those who died in other conflicts. The Royal Exhibition Building, built for the Great Exhibition of 1880 and the seat of Victoria's State Parliament from 1901 until 1927, stands in Carlton Gardens. Melbourne's churches are amongst Australia's most imposing: St Pauls, at the intersection of Flinders and Swanston Streets, is a fine example of Gothic Revival architecture. The Shot Tower, now protected by the dome of Melbourne Central, was used to shape lead shot and pipes.

A CITY OF GREEN SPACES

Melbourne's cool, wet winters and warm summers, its rich alluvial soil and abundant water, are ideal for growing plants, and its parks and gardens are some of Australia's loveliest. The mingling of exotic deciduous trees with Australian natives has produced city gardenscapes that offer foliage colour at all times of the year and brilliant displays of blossom in springtime and summer. Abundant green spaces mean that Melburnians and visitors can look within the city for opportunities to stroll, picnic and enjoy the relief from stress that comes only with closeness to the natural world.

Top: *(Left) A brilliant display of flowers in the Conservatory in Fitzroy Gardens. (Right) Flower gardens blossom in city streets.*
Above: *Green spaces abound close to Melbourne's city centre.*

Above: *An equestrian statue of Edward VII and sumptuous floral clock in Queen Victoria Gardens.*
Below: *(Left) Statues decorate Melbourne's public gardens. (Centre) The Shrine of Remembrance in Kings Domain, with Queen Victoria, Alexandra and Royal Botanic Gardens beyond. (Right) Watching waterfowl in Royal Botanic Gardens.*

Top: *Lygon Street in Carlton is well known for its restaurants and bistros.*
Above: *(Left) Prahran is the site of a popular market. (Right) Melbourne's sidewalk cafés are popular with lunchers and shoppers.*

MELBOURNE HAS FUN

The centre of Melbourne offers a remarkable choice of places to eat and be entertained. In fact, many people say the city is Australia's food capital. The Chinatown area, which follows Little Bourke Street, is home to restaurants large and small featuring cuisines from many nations. Bourke and Collins Streets harbour excellent restaurants, while inner-city Carlton and Fitzroy, Richmond, South Yarra, Prahran and St Kilda offer many places to eat, drink and be merry. Prahran is also home to a great food market. Cinemas, including an IMAX Theatre, abound, and the Melbourne Exhibition Centre on Clarendon Street hosts trade fairs and exhibitions.

Top left and clockwise: *The Ruby Cafe, corner of Brunswick and Johnston Streets; the entrance to Luna Park, St Kilda; hairdresser's sign, Acland Street, St Kilda; environmental street theatre outside the Victorian Arts Centre; the Melbourne Exhibition Centre; inside The Jam Factory, Chapel Street, South Yarra.*

Top left and clockwise: *Collins, Bourke and Swanston are three of Melbourne's major streets; a scene in Swanston St; St Kilda Road, with the Shrine of Remembrance in the background; street-door elegance; a gallery sign; a cherub in Fitzroy Gardens' Conservatory; Captain Cook's parents' cottage, Fitzroy Gardens; Collins Street at night; light-horsemen on parade in Melbourne.*

Melbourne, like other great cities, has its identifying icons. Flinders Street Station, the indomitable Melbourne trams, Princes Bridge, the Melbourne Cricket Ground (known as "the G"), the Princess Theatre, the Queen Victoria Market and the other locations shown on these pages are just a few of the sights that place the viewer firmly in Victoria's gracious capital city.

Top: *(Left) Melbourne Central is a popular shopping venue. (Right) The Princess Theatre, part of the city's cultural life since 1854.*
Above: *A night view across the Yarra River from Southbank, with Queens Bridge and Flinders Street Station at centre right.*

Above: *234 Collins Street, one of Melbourne's most comprehensive retail wonderlands.*

A SHOPPER'S PARADISE

Melbourne's inner city is a shopper's paradise, with department stores, multitudinous shops and retail complexes, exclusive boutiques and specialty outlets. The suburbs all have their own distinctive shopping experiences, from the comprehensive shopping malls that service whole districts to the quirky markets in Prahran, South Melbourne, Footscray and St Kilda. The Queen Victoria Market, on the corner of Victoria and Peel Streets, is over 100 years of age, and is a great place to browse and buy a wide variety of goods, including fresh produce. Connoisseurs of antiques may spend hours in Armadale and surrounding suburbs, while those seeking couture will gravitate to the city's Australia-on-Collins complex, the Bourke Street Mall, Prahran, South Yarra and Toorak, and the bargains of the Richmond fashion warehouses and factory outlets.

Top left and clockwise: *Inside Melbourne Central; Fitzroy Nursery; Royal Arcade, built in 1892, where Gog and Magog strike the hours; seafood stall at Queen Victoria Market; Chadstone Shopping Centre; the Block Arcade, built in 1890.*

CREATURES GREAT AND SMALL

Two of Melbourne's foremost attractions are in easy reach of the city centre. One is the marvellous Melbourne Aquarium, just down the Yarra River from Flinders Walk. Inside are fascinating displays of marine life, featuring life on coral reefs, in mangroves and in Port Phillip Bay. There is shark-feeding, an Ocean Theatre and a sensational walk-through tunnel that takes the visitor into the heart of the sea creatures' habitat.

Just outside the city area in spacious Royal Park, the Royal Melbourne Zoological Gardens displays around 400 species of native and exotic animals in habitats that give the residents stimulation and comfort. Popular exhibits include the breeding colony of gorillas, the otters frolicking in their glass-sided pool, stately giraffes, a Butterfly House, a Reptile House and the Great Flight Aviary. Melbourne Zoo has a free-range counterpart at Werribee, just west of the city.

Top: *The impressive and popular Melbourne Aquarium is sited on the Yarra River.*
Above: *(Left) The Leafy Seadragon is a popular exhibit. (Right) Sharks star in the aquarium's Ocean Theatre.*

Some scenes from Melbourne's Royal Zoological Gardens. **Top left and clockwise:** *Giraffe; Snow Leopard; Short-clawed Otters; one of the zoo's breeding colony of Lowland Gorillas; a popular statue of an elephant in one of the zoo's lovely gardens.*

Above: *They're off! The start of another memorable Melbourne Cup at Flemington Racecourse.*

Below: *(Left) A Test Match fills the Melbourne Cricket Ground with spectators. (Right) A triumphant moment at Albert Park during the Australian Formula One Grand Prix.*

Above: *Australian Rules Football is Melbourne's most popular spectator sport, dominating autumn and winter weekends.*

MAD ABOUT SPORT

Name your spectator sport and it is sure to be played in Melbourne and attract a dedicated following. Cricket draws the crowds throughout summer, while for two weeks in January the world's best tennis players battle out the Australian Open at Melbourne Park. In March, the Australian Formula One Grand Prix sends cars racing around Albert Park Lake. In October, the big bikes roar around the seaside circuit on Phillip Island in the Australian Motorcycle Grand Prix, a round in the 500cc World Championship. For horse-racing enthusiasts, the Spring Carnival, which ends on a high on the first Tuesday of November with the Melbourne Cup, is a festival of delight. However, Melbourne is, above all, a football town. Soccer is popular, and Melbourne Storm lives up to its name in the national Rugby League competition. But the game that dominates is Aussie Rules, the born-by-the-Yarra, 100 minutes or so of athletic spectacle that is a weekly game in the Australian Football League season.

Top: *The Bolte Bridge.* **Above:** *West Gate Bridge carries traffic across the Yarra to the south-western suburbs and Geelong.*
Opposite: *(Top left) The footbridge connecting Southgate to Flinders Walk. (Top right) Princes Bridge.*
(Centre) West Gate Bridge at dusk. (Bottom) Swan Street Bridge.

A CITY OF BRIDGES

As the Yarra meanders through Melbourne to Port Phillip Bay, it is crossed by a number of bridges. These range from the classic, elegant, stone constructions of Kings, Queens and Princes Bridges to the airy, modernistic curve of the footbridge linking Southgate with Flinders Walk. Mightiest of all are the Bolte Bridge and the massive West Gate Bridge, which, at 2582 metres with a 336-metre span across the river, is longer than Sydney Harbour Bridge. Beneath this bridge and its approaches are fresh and saltwater lakes that abound in birdlife and form West Gate Park.

Top: *An aerial view of Brighton, a popular bayside suburb.* **Above:** *Colourful bathing boxes border the beach at Brighton.*
Below: *(Left) Sailing and powerboating are popular on Port Phillip Bay. (Right) Cycling is a great way to exercise along the shores of Port Phillip.*

PORT PHILLIP BAY: A CITY'S PLAYGROUND

The city of Melbourne was founded on the northern shore of Port Phillip Bay. Today the urban area has spread right around the bay's northern curve and down its eastern and western shores to the Mornington and Bellarine Peninsulas. The 264-kilometre shoreline of Port Phillip Bay is sheltered from the turbulence of the open sea, and the bay's waters offer magnificent fishing, swimming and boating, although navigational challenges are not lacking. These waters abound in marine life: recent programs have undertaken to study this valuable resource and keep it viable. The bayside suburbs nearest the city heart – Port Melbourne, Albert Park, Middle Park, St Kilda and Brighton – provide recreational facilities for city folk: watersports, seaside delights and a dazzling mix of waterside activities that include rollerblading, cycling, walking and jogging. These suburbs are also treasure-houses of cafés, restaurants, bistros, street markets and entertainments, theatre, picnic facilities and promenades such as the much-loved St Kilda Pier.

Top: *(Left) Aerial view of St Kilda, the marina and pier. (Right) Promenaders throng St Kilda Pier.*
Above: *Melbourne's city skyline seen through a forest of masts on St Kilda Harbour.*

Above: *A view across Williamstown Marina and the suburb itself to Port Phillip Bay.*

HISTORIC WILLIAMSTOWN

Way back in 1837, the new town of Melbourne was envisaged as being the city, and Williamstown, just south of the Yarra mouth on the western side of Hobsons Bay, the seaport. Services such as customs and immigration were set up in Williamstown, and impressive buildings of local stone were erected. The bluestone Timeball Tower signalled one o'clock in the afternoon, so ships' masters could set the chronometers which were used to navigate at sea.

In the 1880s, the Port of Melbourne was developed and Williamstown was neglected for many years. Today it is a bayside suburb of charm and historical interest, with many of Nelson Place's buildings listed by the National Trust. A multitude of pleasure craft moor along the seafront.

Williamstown can be reached by road across West Gate Bridge, and by train or ferry. On the way, not far past the bridge, visitors can explore the hands-on delights of the Scienceworks Museum.

Top left and clockwise: *Pleasure craft in Williamstown Marina; the Timeball Tower signalled the time, helping ships' masters set their chronometers; hands-on displays at Scienceworks, Spotswood; Nelson Place, Williamstown, offers cafés, restaurants and shopping in its refurbished nineteenth-century buildings; enjoying the bayside air.*

Top: *(Left) Olivers Hill at popular Frankston. (Right) Hastings Boat Harbour.* **Above:** *Relaxing on a peaceful beach at Blairgowrie.*
Below: *(Left) Point Nepean, the tip of the Mornington Peninsula. (Right) Cape Schanck, southernmost prominence on the Bass Strait aspect of the peninsula.*

Above: *The Mornington Peninsula — a haven of safe moorings and seaside pleasures in the waters of Port Phillip Bay.*

THE MORNINGTON PENINSULA

Stretching down the eastern side of Port Phillip Bay, the Mornington Peninsula has been a refuge and playground for Melburnians for around 130 years. Today, the seaside resorts have become towns in their own right and the city is creeping southwards, but the peninsula still offers plenty for holiday-makers. The "front" beaches on the Port Phillip side are ideal for families, while the Bass Strait "back" beaches are wilder and more challenging. Walking tracks allow access to some glorious coastal spots: Mornington Peninsula National Park protects bushland and wildlife from Point Nepean on the western tip of the peninsula to Cape Schanck on its south-eastern point. Many vacationers spend their time checking out restaurants, wineries and antique shops, all of which abound on the peninsula.

Very few of the world's cities have such easy access to green places as Melbourne, and the Dandenong Ranges, only 50 kilometres east of the city, contain some of Australia's loveliest forest. The Dandenongs have been a magnet for city-dwellers for well over a century. However, today it is still possible to hike along trails in the Dandenong Ranges National Park without meeting another soul, awed by magnificent stands of Mountain Ash, hearing the ventriloquial mimicry of the Superb Lyrebird resound from the gullies. Garden enthusiasts are drawn to the ranges by public gardens such as the splendid Olinda Rhododendron Gardens and the William Ricketts Sanctuary, with its sculptured figures. Dandenongs towns offer hospitality, galleries and craft boutiques, and no visit would be complete without a ride on the historic steam train Puffing Billy, which travels from Belgrave to Emerald Lake and back again.

Top: *Puffing Billy, a restored steam engine, runs between Belgrave, Emerald Lakeside Park and Gembrook.*
Above: *(Left) National Rhododendron Gardens at Olinda. (Right) Statue in the William Ricketts Sanctuary.*

Top left and clockwise: *Common Wombat; Platypus; Koala and young one; a Dingo and admirers at Healesville.*

HEALESVILLE SANCTUARY

Only 65 kilometres along the Maroondah Highway from Melbourne, Healesville Sanctuary is an ideal place to meet Australia's wildlife at close quarters. The sanctuary is more than just a zoo; it carries out research into wild creatures of many sorts and is committed to breeding endangered species as well as promoting public understanding of native animals and their habitats. Opened in 1934, Healesville includes plenty of creekside bushland where visitors can wander through a multitude of fascinating displays. Highlights of a Healesville visit are close-up encounters with Dingos, Common Wombats, Koalas and Platypuses, as well as Australian Pelican feeding and spectacular flights by birds of prey.

Above: *(Left) A pair of Little Penguins in their nest. (Right) A Little Penguin waddling up the beach.*
Below: *Phillip Island coastline from the Nobbies.*

Top: *The circuit where the Australian Motorcycle Grand Prix is held.*
Above: *Action in the 500cc Motorcycle Grand Prix.*

DELIGHTS OF PHILLIP ISLAND

Only 125 kilometres south-east of Melbourne at the entrance to Western Port, Phillip Island is famous for its beaches – the rugged southern ones are noted for great surf. Summerland Beach on the south-west point attracts large crowds to its "penguin parade" just after sunset. Flocks of Little Penguins leave the sea to waddle to their nests. Other island wildlife includes Australian Fur-seals and Koalas. Each October the Australian Motorcycle Grand Prix provides thrills for racing fans.

Scenes from Wilsons Promontory National Park, a wilderness area within easy reach of Melbourne.
Top: (Left) The view from Mt Oberon. (Right) Whisky Bay. **Above:** Squeaky Beach.

EAST OF MELBOURNE

Wilsons Promontory, a national park since 1905, is about 170 kilometres south-east of Melbourne. "The Prom" is magnificent – its abundant wildlife, rugged headlands, sandy beaches, flowering heathland and rainforest gullies appeal particularly to nature-lovers and bushwalkers. Further along the South Gippsland Highway, the water wonderland of the Gippsland Lakes and Ninety Mile Beach border fertile pastures. North-eastern Victoria is dominated by the Great Dividing Range, snowclad in winter and a mecca for bushwalkers and wilderness adventurers in summer.

Top left and clockwise: *A boardwalk through rainforest at Marysville in the Central Highlands; snow on the Victorian Alps; the Gippsland Lakes, separated from the ocean by the silver sand of Ninety Mile Beach; autumn foliage near Bright.*

Top left and clockwise: *Viewing the Grampians from the Jaws of Death (also known as The Balconies); climbing at Mt Arapiles; Erskine Falls, Angahook-Lorne State Park; fishing from the jetty at Queenscliff; surfboards at Anglesea; Proudfoots Hopkins River Boathouse at Warrnambool.*

WEST OF MELBOURNE

The Bellarine Peninsula, the western arm of land embracing Port Phillip Bay, has a long association with the sea, and the town of Queenscliff is popular with fishers and divers. Westward along the coast are some of Australia's best surf beaches and most spectacular coastal scenery, accessible by the Great Ocean Road. Dedicated to the dead of World War I, this was constructed by ex-servicemen between 1918 and 1932, and now takes travellers along the southern coast and across the rainforests of the Otway Ranges. In western Victoria, the grandeur of the Grampians and the challenging sandstone pitches of Mt Arapiles provide stark contrast to the pastoral and grain-growing areas that stretch northwards to the dry but wildlife-rich country south of the Murray River.

Above: *The Twelve Apostles are imposing limestone stacks that rise from the ocean in Port Campbell National Park.*

Victoria is Australia's smallest mainland State, occupying less than 3% of the nation's total area, but it encompasses a wide variety of landscapes. North of Melbourne the fertile land supports vineyards, cattle and sheep farms, and many country towns. From Ballarat to Bendigo, through Daylesford and Hepburn Springs to Castlemaine, old gold mining towns still resound with the echoes of the rush days. At the northernmost edge of the State, the Murray River forms a picturesque and useful border with New South Wales.

Top: (Left) A peaceful pastoral scene in central Victoria. (Right) A Cobb & Co coach carries passengers at Sovereign Hill, Ballarat.
Above: A paddlewheeler on the Murray brings back memories of the roaring days when this great river was alive with such craft.